MOST WANTED

The Revolutionary Partnership of
JOHN HANCOCK & SAMUEL ADAMS

By SARAH JANE MARSH

Illustrated by EDWIN FOTHERINGHAM

DISNEP • HYPERION
LOS ANGELES   NEW YORK

*The author would like to share deep appreciation for historian
J. L. Bell, editor Rotem Moscovich, assistant editor Heather Crowley,
illustrator Edwin Fotheringham, art designer Phil Buchanan,
the entire team at Disney Hyperion, agent Caryn Wiseman, Martha
Brockenbrough, Mark Correira, and the Diversity Jedi.*

First Edition, March 2020
10 9 8 7 6 5 4 3 2 1
FAC- 029191-20038
Printed in Malaysia

This book is set in 14-point Shipley Regular, Shipley Rough,
Mailart Rubberstamp, 1726 Real Espanola Regular, The Redlight/Fontspring
Designed by Phil Buchanan

Library of Congress Control Number: 2019945149

ISBN 978-1-368-02683-3

Reinforced binding
Visit www.DisneyBooks.com

To my most wanted:
Elsa, Faith, Noah, and Mark —S.J.M.

For my family, as ever —E.F.

$\mathcal{J}$ohn Hancock was rich. He owned ships and stores, warehouses and wharves, and lived in a mansion with fifty-four windows high above Boston.

He rode around town in a golden carriage pulled by four gleaming horses.

His wig—powdered.

His shirts—ruffled.

His shoe buckles—sparkling.

Samuel Adams was outspoken. He owned very little—not even one horse. He strode around town talking politics with silversmiths and sailors, wigmakers and whalers, and the tenors and basses in his church choir. His hair un-powdered, shirts shabby, and shoes worn thin.

Adams was proud to be an American colonist. His family had lived in Massachusetts for five generations. He loved to discuss American liberty and the law.

Hancock loved parties and peach trees!
He loved praise and personal attention!
He loved fashion and fine wine
"*at any price.*" After Hancock
was seen strutting in a suit
of red velvet, it was
rumored a West Newbury
doctor walked thirty
miles just to purchase
a similar cloth.

It was terribly flattering.

Hancock had a Harvard education, and his elite family status
had placed him first in line for chocolate and biscuits at breakfast.

Adams had a Harvard education, too. But when he was nineteen,
Parliament—the royal government of Great Britain—passed
a law that closed his father's colonial bank,
declared it "*illegal*," and left the family
in financial distress.

It was terribly unfair.

Adams grew up contemplating his colonial rights. "*The true object of loyalty,*" he said, "*is a good legal constitution.*"

Hancock grew up contemplating his closet. "*I am obliged,*" he said, "*to be pretty expensive.*"

One day,
Britain's Parliament
decided to tax the American
colonists to raise money. They ordered a stamp
tax on nearly every piece of printed paper: licenses and
legal documents, pamphlets and newspapers, even playing cards.
Hancock found the new law *very cruel,* but agreed *we must
submit to higher powers.*

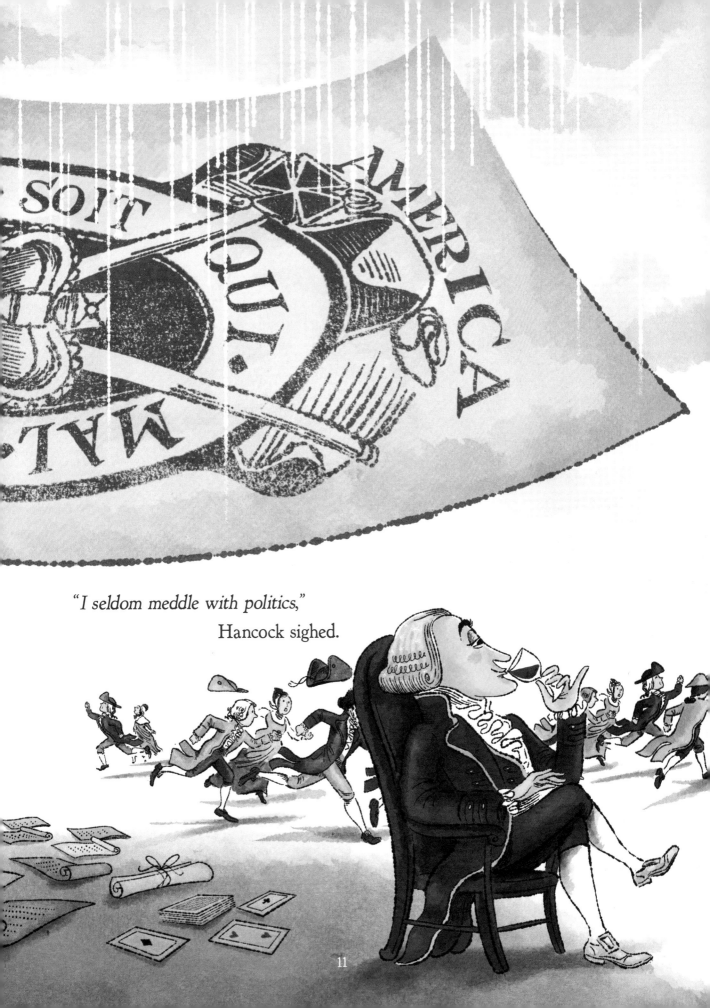

"*I seldom meddle with politics,*"
        Hancock sighed.

11

Adams, however, found the new law "*unconstitutional*" and "*alarming*." Parliament had NO RIGHT to tax the colonists—the colonies had always taxed themselves! If they didn't defend their rights and liberties, where would Parliament stop?

So Adams stormed around town, stirring up opposition
in meetings, letters, and newspapers, urging the people
"to declare our greatest dissatisfaction with this law."

The stamp tax sparked an uproar throughout the colonies. One night, an angry mob attacked the homes of Boston's wealthy royal officials, smashing furniture and shattering windows.

Hancock was shocked. He might be next *"to lose my property, if not my life."*

Adams also disapproved of the violence. But he saw an opportunity to recruit Boston's wealthiest and most visible citizen to the cause. Might Hancock be willing to join a peaceful boycott of British goods, Adams asked him?

Why yes, yes he would. With a flourish of his pen, Hancock the merchant became Hancock— the patriot.

And he liked it.

Before long, newspapers praised Hancock for being "*first*" to boldly send a ship to London without paying the royal tax.

"I will not be a slave," he boasted.
"I have a right to the liberties and
privileges of the English constitution,
and I as an Englishman will enjoy them."

Soon, the young and dashing Hancock was seen alongside old and stodgy Adams, rallying the people against Britain's unfair law.

They made a very persuasive pair:
Adams led the conversation; Hancock paid the bill!
Adams had firm opinions; Hancock had flair!

Boycotts and protests against the stamp tax raged up and down the colonies. And their resistance worked. Parliament agreed to repeal the offending law, and Boston went wild with celebration. Bands marched, flags flew, and fireworks lit up the night sky. From his mansion on Beacon Hill, Hancock blasted his own fireworks, dazzling the crowd, and provided free wine for everyone.

Riding a wave of popularity, Hancock and Adams became leaders of the Boston Town Meeting and the Massachusetts colonial legislature.

After Hancock won his first big election, Samuel Adams took a stroll with his cousin John Adams. *"The town has done a wise thing today,"* he said, pointing to Hancock's stately mansion. *"They have made that young man's fortune their own."*

It was true. Inspired by his new leadership role, Hancock gave generously to the people of Boston—and to the patriot cause. He provided free food and firewood to the poor, bought bells and bibles for churches, and outfitted the town with the latest fire engine. And he paid for patriot celebrations, where, of course, he sat first at the table.

The people adored him. "*Mr. Hancock*," John Adams said, "*was the delight of the eyes of the whole town.*"

But their troubles were far from over. For ten years, Britain tried to tighten its grip on the colonies with tough new laws. Parliament ordered a tax on glass, lead, paper, paint, and tea. They sent soldiers and tax collectors to enforce the king's law. And they declared their authority over the colonists *in all cases whatsoever.*

Sons of Liberty

And for ten years, Hancock and Adams led the resistance in Boston.

John Hancock rebelled with enthusiasm—and elegance:

He signed dissenting documents. . . .

      He led meetings and liberty parades. . . .

           And he gave a manly speech with a penetrating gaze and a determined chin.

Samuel Adams was relentless. He organized protests and processions, demonstrations and displays. He wrote letters and petitions and articles and essays. And he gathered people into meetings and committees and associations to safeguard their liberties against the unfair and unfeeling government of Great Britain.

When British soldiers fired into a threatening crowd of angry
colonists, killing five, Adams led the town-wide effort to demand justice
for the *"horrid massacre."*

Working together, Hancock and Adams formed a powerful partnership. And at times when Hancock pouted over politics, threatening to quit, Adams gently coaxed him back on course, reminding his *"affectionate friend"* he was *"most valuable"* and worthy of *"the highest applause."*

It was exhausting. John Hancock once went sailing up the coast of Maine just to relax.

Samuel Adams never relaxed. He was always "cooking up
Paragraphs ... working the political Engine!" When people
saw a light shining late at night from his upstairs window, they
knew it was Adams "hard at work writing against the Tories."

And his words traveled far.

They circulated throughout Massachusetts, up and down the colonies, and across the sea to London, where they were read as "*The True Sentiments of America.*"

"*Every dip of his pen stung like a horned snake,*"
grumbled the royal governor.

The vigilant voice of Samuel Adams was becoming
the official opinion of an unhappy America.

And the daring disobedience of John Hancock was becoming
the inspiring image of a defiant America.

When royal officers tried to inspect his ship *Lydia*, Hancock
tossed them off.

When they tried to inspect his ship *Liberty*, Hancock's captain locked them in the hold.

And when the Royal Navy seized the *Liberty* as punishment, an angry crowd rioted through Boston in Hancock's defense.

Hancock was "an *idol of the mob*," wailed the officers.

Together, Hancock and Adams were becoming a royal pain.

Finally, when Britain refused to remove a tax on tea, Hancock and Adams held a town meeting with 5,000 of their angriest friends.

"This meeting can

"Let every man

do nothing more!"

announced Adams.

do what is right!"

hollered Hancock.

The next morning, over 92,000 pounds of fine British tea were found floating in Boston Harbor.

Across the ocean in London, King George was not amused. His American colonies were behaving very badly. They had ignored his laws, terrorized his tax collectors, harassed his soldiers, boycotted his trade, and sent a flurry of disobedient letters into his royal lap.

And now they had tossed his tea.

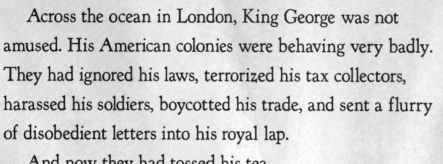

"Violent and outrageous!"

"Punish Hancock [and] Adams!" cried Parliament. "The town of Boston ought to be knocked about their ears and destroyed!"

Parliament ordered:

Boston Harbor—closed.

Massachusetts town meetings—restricted.

The Massachusetts colonial government—revoked.

And to enforce the king's law, they marched more soldiers into the streets of Boston under the command of General Thomas Gage—the new royal governor of Massachusetts.

There would be no more monkey business in Boston.

Adams was outraged. He locked the door of the legislature and called for an emergency meeting of all the colonies. *"ALL should be united in opposition to this violation of the liberties of ALL."*

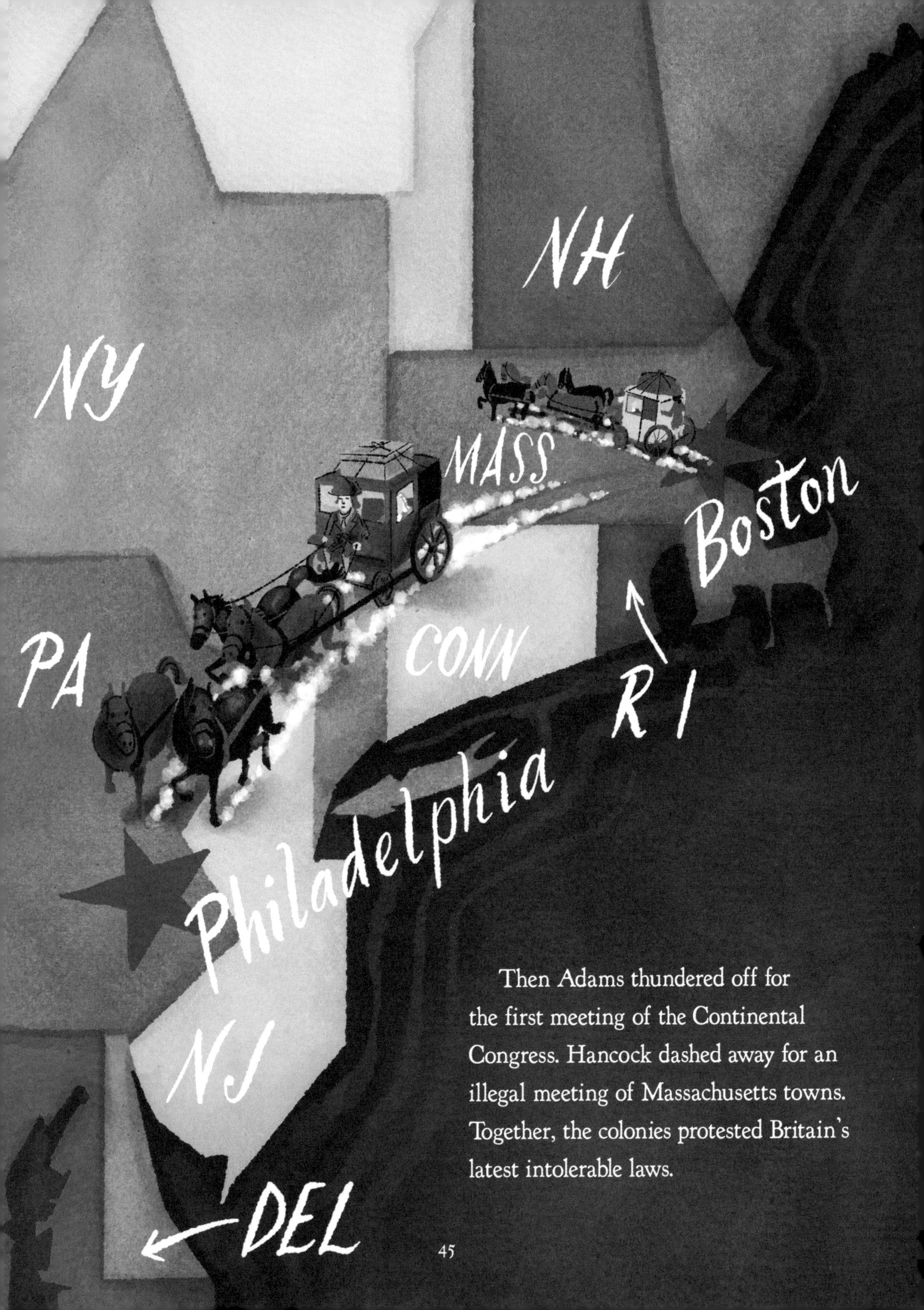

NH

NY

MASS

Boston

PA

CONN

RI

Philadelphia

NJ

DEL

45

Then Adams thundered off for
the first meeting of the Continental
Congress. Hancock dashed away for an
illegal meeting of Massachusetts towns.
Together, the colonies protested Britain's
latest intolerable laws.

But their defiance only made their royal government more angry.

Britain ordered more soldiers and generals and warships to Massachusetts.

"*Criminal!*"

Massachusetts gathered cannon and gunpowder and militia to defend themselves. *"It is our duty at all hazards to preserve the public liberty!"* warned Adams. *"Be ready to take the field whenever danger calls!"* cried Hancock.

King George fumed. It was time to end this pesky rebellion once and for all. He ordered General Gage to crush the *"daring spirit of resistance"* in Massachusetts.

"Treason and rebellion!" cried Parliament.

Rumors spread throughout the colonies. A warship was on its way with orders for General Gage to arrest "*the most obnoxious of the leaders*" and force Massachusetts to obey.

Dread set in over the town of Boston. More punishment was coming. Even Benjamin Franklin worried for "*the most notorious offenders . . . Hancock [and] Adams.*"

Should they leave town for a while?
Adams asked Hancock.

Why yes, yes they should.

The two rebel leaders packed their bags and hurried off to the quiet village of Lexington. They would stay with Hancock's country cousins—a family of eleven.

The house was not so quiet.

Meanwhile, Boston waited nervously as the warship arrived. A British officer scurried to deliver General Gage his new orders.

General Gage pondered the lengthy letter. He must take action to disarm the colonists and restore the king's authority. Looking over his spy reports, General Gage made a secret plan.

Would he arrest Hancock and Adams? Would he seize and destroy the rebel supplies in the town of Concord, out past Lexington?

Several nights later, his officers were seen riding toward Lexington, armed with pistols.

All around the countryside, patriots alarmed into action.

The Committee of Safety sent Hancock a hastily scribbled warning.

The Lexington militia arrived to guard the house.

And at midnight, a breathless messenger from Boston clattered to a halt and demanded to enter.

Hancock flung open a window
and peered out into the night.
"Come in, Revere," Hancock called.
"We are not afraid of you!"
Paul Revere tromped into the house with
more concerning news.

"The Regulars are coming out!"

In the dead of night, General Gage's army had secretly left Boston and was marching this way!

John Hancock—rebel in ruffles—realized danger was calling. He polished his pistol. He sharpened his sword. He was determined to take the field and fight.

"*That is not our business*," replied Adams.
The discussion took hours.

Hancock agreed to escape with Adams. "*If I had my musket,*" he declared, "*I would never turn my back upon these troops!*"

Then he turned his back, climbed into his golden carriage, and fled.

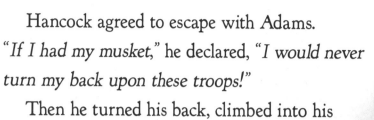

As the sun began to rise, General Gage's soldiers marched into sight.

Hancock and Adams hid as fighting broke out between General Gage's army and colonial militiamen in Lexington and then Concord. Under constant gunfire, Gage's army retreated to Boston, blasting cannons and burning houses, leaving behind chaos and bloodshed.

Hancock and Adams had little time to think. They were due to depart for the next meeting of the Continental Congress.

Would the other colonies blame Massachusetts for leading them into war?
Would Hancock and Adams be arrested along the way?

This time, had they gone too far?

Anxiously, Hancock and Adams began their journey to
Philadelphia. Twelve armed men rode alongside to keep them safe.
The rebel leaders from Massachusetts had become outlaws.
And Hancock didn't like it.

But as they traveled south, so did the news of Lexington and Concord. The rabble-rousing colonists of Massachusetts had defended their American liberties with their lives.

And one by one, people began to line the streets . . . and cheer.

Boston

New York

New Jersey

Philadelphia

68

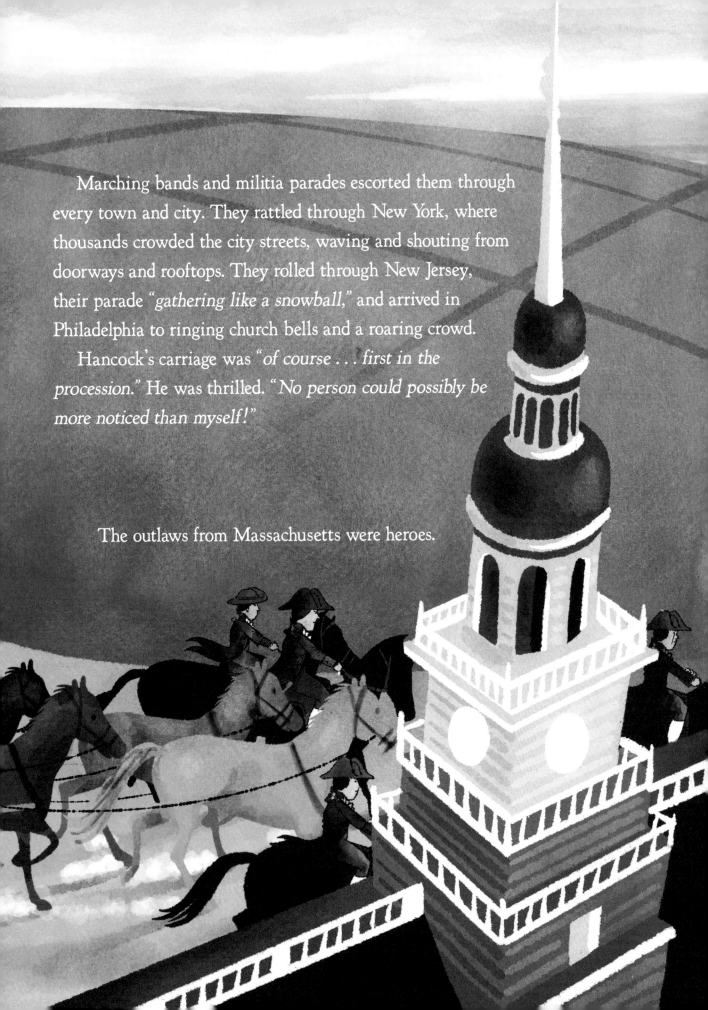

Marching bands and militia parades escorted them through every town and city. They rattled through New York, where thousands crowded the city streets, waving and shouting from doorways and rooftops. They rolled through New Jersey, their parade *"gathering like a snowball,"* and arrived in Philadelphia to ringing church bells and a roaring crowd.

Hancock's carriage was *"of course . . . first in the procession."* He was thrilled. *"No person could possibly be more noticed than myself!"*

The outlaws from Massachusetts were heroes.

Meanwhile, back in Boston, surrounded by fifteen thousand armed
and angry militia, General Gage contemplated his disastrous situation.

His secret plans—failed.

The American people—outraged.

His entire army—trapped.

Instead of crushing the resistance, they had ignited a war.

In one last attempt to regain control, he dipped his pen in
ink and issued a proclamation:

*"I do hereby in his Majesty's name, offer
and promise his most gracious pardon to
all persons who shall forthwith lay down
their arms, and return to the duties of
peaceable subjects, excepting only . . .*

It was official. Hancock and Adams were now Britain's most wanted. Together, the patriot heroes from Boston had become the defining image of a determined people.

And together, the people contemplated their future.

The American Revolution had begun.

Don't Forget the Salmon! (Where Did Hancock and Adams Hide?)

After arriving in Lexington, Hancock invited his elderly aunt, Lydia Hancock, and his fiancée, Dorothy ("Dolly") Quincy, to join him at the Clarke home—for several weeks—while he and Adams attended nearby meetings of the Massachusetts Provincial Congress. With fifteen people in the little house, it must have been terribly crowded!

According to Dolly, a local citizen gave the household a *"fine salmon"* for dinner. But before it could be cooked, Paul Revere (and, later, fellow messenger William Dawes) arrived to warn that Gage's army was heading their way. Eventually Hancock was persuaded to flee with Adams to the town of Woburn and hide at the home of the town minister.

Meanwhile, the Clarke family and their guests watched as fighting broke out between British soldiers and Lexington militia on the town common. After Gage's army marched away to Concord, the household cared for two wounded militiamen and hurried to hide their valuables and evacuate the children before the army returned.

What was Hancock thinking about during this time? Apparently, his lunch. Hancock sent his carriage back to Lexington with a message for Dolly and Aunt Lydia to *"get into the carriage and come over, and bring the fine salmon."* The ladies grabbed the fish and rumbled off to Woburn.

There, everyone prepared to sit down to a tasty feast. But before they could take a bite, another messenger burst through the door, warning Hancock and Adams to flee yet again. Gage's army was dangerously close, battling their way back to Boston.

Hancock and Adams bolted out of the house and into the woods. They hurried to the town of Billerica, finding refuge in the home of Mrs. Wyman, already crowded with fleeing women and children.

Hancock was still hungry. Mrs. Wyman offered the finest food she could provide—cold pork and boiled potatoes. According to Dolly, Hancock later repaid Mrs. Wyman for her hospitality by gifting her a cow.

More to the Story . . .

Were Hancock and Adams Ever in Danger?

People at the time believed both men would be arrested. For over a year, friends in London (including Benjamin Franklin) had warned of discussions to arrest Hancock, Adams, and other ringleaders. In anticipation, Gage's soldiers began threatening rebel leaders around Boston. In Lexington, Hancock's cousin worried that *"sudden arrest, if not assassination, might be attempted."*

Why Didn't General Gage Arrest Hancock and Adams?

Although Gage's orders advised him to arrest rebel leaders and disarm the colonists, he was also told to use his own judgment. No evidence exists that Gage planned to capture Hancock and Adams—his instructions to his officers don't mention arresting anyone at all. Later, he gave an excuse: *"It was too late. They had received timely notice of their danger and were fled."* Gage likely understood better than his superiors in London that the rebellion was a mass movement of the people against British colonial policies. Arresting Hancock and Adams would do little to stop it.

74

Why Did General Gage's Army March to Concord?

It was well known that the Provincial Congress was collecting military supplies in Concord. To Gage's embarrassment, colonists had also smuggled four prized cannon out of Boston. Gage needed to take action. Colonists suspected he might try to recover the supplies in Concord. Paul Revere rode out to warn the town on April 16, two days before his famous midnight ride. (Revere made many rides.) Concord hurried to hide its weapons, and Gage's attempt to disarm the colonists ended in disaster.

What Happened to the Four Cannon?

Two cannon were recaptured by the British army during the Revolutionary War. In 1788, the U.S. Congress gifted its two remaining cannon to Boston, where Secretary of War Henry Knox proudly named them "Hancock" and "Adams."

Why Did the Lexington Militia Stand Against the British Army?

Although Massachusetts readied its militia for the possibility of war, the fighting in Lexington and Concord was not planned. (To this day, we don't know who fired the first shot in Lexington. The guns at the time were unreliable, so it's possible the first shot was accidental.) The Massachusetts Provincial Congress had ordered local militias to take a stand *"whenever the army under command of General Gage . . . to the number of five hundred, shall march out of Boston, with artillery and baggage. . . ."* This was likely on the mind of the Lexington militia that morning.

Were Hancock and Adams Ever Arrested?

No. Both men were safe in Philadelphia for the Second Continental Congress when General Gage published his proclamation. Five days later, the British Army (reinforced with three newly arrived generals) attacked the colonists surrounding Boston in the Battle of Bunker Hill. Everyone's attention turned toward war.

John Hancock's Famous Signature

In many ways, John Hancock's flamboyant nature and defiant acts made him America's first celebrity. Today Hancock is best known for his bold and elegant signature on the Declaration of Independence. In fact, the term "John Hancock" can be found in the dictionary as a synonym for "signature." Was Hancock's oversized signature another sign of his oversized ego? Probably not. As president of the Continental Congress, he often signed public documents along with Secretary Charles Thomson, so a large and centered signature was appropriate. For almost a month, theirs were the only names attached to the Declaration of Independence, until other members of Congress began adding their signatures in August 1776.

Author's Note

I began work on *Most Wanted* in 2015, initially drawn to chaotic events at the Clarke house on April 18, 1775. Over time, my story expanded to the legendary partnership of John Hancock and Samuel Adams across ten years. Even as I wrote, I continued to learn. Hancock and Adams were part of a broader story. The revolution was a mass movement of the people—a remarkable feat of grassroots organizing by ordinary citizens who rose to meet the challenges of their time. This is the history that gets celebrated. This is the story I wrote through the lens of Hancock and Adams.

But as I write this note in 2019, I've learned my own lens was faulty. The origin story of the United States is complex and contradictory. And it is not all to be celebrated. My blind spots as an author perpetuate a history that is narrow and incomplete. There is much more to the story. Although they complained of being enslaved by British taxation policies, all thirteen colonies supported the practice of slavery. Hancock enslaved several people. While the colonies demanded liberty from Britain, they denied rights to women, African Americans, Native Americans, and others not included in the founders' declaration that *"all men are created equal."* And while Americans celebrated the birth of their new nation, they were trying to extinguish the existence of Native nations already inhabiting the lands they sought to colonize.

So how does America reconcile a patriotic pride in its revolutionary roots with the violence and human suffering inflicted in this history? These are important questions with which we must wrestle. History surrounds us still.

My understanding of these issues is just beginning, thanks to the work of many courageous and deeply knowledgeable people drawing attention to the lives and experiences often left out of our books and stories. These omissions distort our history, and as a result—our understanding of ourselves. As you read *Most Wanted*, I invite you to engage critically with the text. Question my perspective. Discuss whose stories are told and whose are not. And seek resources to expand your learning, some of which I've shared on my website. Together, our learning continues.

Timeline

September 16, 1722

Samuel Adams is born in Boston, Massachusetts.

1736–40

Adams attends Harvard College.

January 12, 1737

John Hancock is born in Braintree (now Quincy), Massachusetts.

1741

Parliament declares Adams's father's Land Bank illegal.

1744

Hancock's father dies. Hancock is adopted by his aunt and uncle and moves to Boston.

1749

Adams marries Elizabeth Checkley. They have six children, but only two survive infancy. Elizabeth dies after childbirth in 1757.

1750–4

Hancock attends Harvard College.

1756

The town of Boston appoints Adams to collect local taxes.

1763

The French and Indian War ends. Hancock becomes a partner in his uncle's merchant business.

1764

Hancock's uncle Thomas dies. Hancock inherits his business and estate.

Adams marries Elizabeth Wells.

1765

Britain passes the Stamp Act.

Adams is elected to the Massachusetts legislature. Hancock is elected Boston selectman.

1766

Britain repeals the Stamp Act and passes the Declaratory Act.

Hancock is elected to the Massachusetts colonial legislature.

1767

Parliament approves the Townshend Acts, taxing the colonists on glass, lead, paper, paint, and tea from Britain.

1768

Adams authors a letter from the Massachusetts legislature to other colonies, encouraging resistance to the Townshend Acts.

Royal customs officials seize Hancock's ship *Liberty*.

British troops arrive in Boston to enforce the Townshend Acts.

1770

Britain repeals the Townshend Acts, except for a tax on tea.

Five colonists are killed in a brawl with British soldiers, later called the Boston Massacre.

Adams organizes a funeral procession with ten thousand people, and writes twenty-six thousand words in the newspaper about the subsequent court trial. His cousin John Adams is a defense attorney for the British soldiers.

1772

Adams leads the creation of Boston's Committee of Correspondence.

1773

Bostonians protest the Tea Act by dumping British tea into Boston Harbor. The event is known today as the Boston Tea Party.

1774

Hancock delivers Boston's annual Massacre Day speech.

As punishment for the Boston Tea Party, Parliament passes the Coercive Acts. Also known today as the Intolerable Acts.

Adams attends the First Continental Congress in Philadelphia.

Hancock attends the first Massachusetts Provincial Congress, where he is elected president.

1775

The Battle of Lexington and Concord occurs on April 19.

Hancock and Adams attend the Second Continental Congress in Philadelphia. Hancock is voted president.

General Gage issues a proclamation on June 12 exempting Hancock and Adams from pardon.

British troops attack colonial forces at the Battle of Bunker Hill on June 17.

Hancock marries Dorothy ("Dolly") Quincy. They later have two children, who both die in childhood.

1776

Thomas Paine publishes *Common Sense*, advocating for American independence.

Congress approves a written Declaration of Independence on July 4.

1780

Hancock is elected the first governor of Massachusetts.

1781

Adams leaves the Continental Congress to preside over the Massachusetts State Senate.

1783

The war ends with the Treaty of Paris on September 3.

1789

Adams is elected lieutenant governor under Governor Hancock.

October 8, 1793

After serving nine terms as governor of Massachusetts, Hancock dies at home of illness at age fifty-seven.

1794

Adams is elected governor of Massachusetts.

1797

Adams retires from public service at age seventy-five.

October 2, 1803

Adams dies at home of old age at eighty-one.

Selected Bibliography

Adams, Samuel. *The Writings of Samuel Adams* (Vols. 1–3). Edited by Harry Alonzo Cushing. New York: G. P. Putnam's Sons, 1904–7.

Bell, J. L. *The Road to Concord*. Yardley, PA: Westholme, 2016.

Brown, Abram English. *John Hancock: His Book*. Boston: Lee and Shepard, 1898.

Carp, Benjamin L. *Defiance of the Patriots*. New Haven: Yale University Press, 2010.

Carter, Clarence Edwin, ed. *The Correspondence of General Thomas Gage*. New Haven: Yale University Press, 1933.

Fischer, David Hackett. *Paul Revere's Ride*. New York: Oxford University Press, 1994.

Fowler, William M. *Samuel Adams: Radical Puritan*. New York: Addison-Wesley, 1997.

Kollen, Richard. *The Patriot Parson of Lexington, Massachusetts*. Charleston, SC: The History Press, 2016.

Maier, Pauline. "Coming to Terms with Samuel Adams," *The American Historical Review*. Vol. 81:1. February 1976.

Raphael, Ray, and Marie Raphael. *The Spirit of '74*. New York: New Press, 2015.

Stoll, Ira. *Samuel Adams: A Life*. New York: Free Press, 2008.

Tourtellot, Arthur B. *Lexington and Concord*. New York: W. W. Norton & Company, 1959.

Unger, Harlow Giles. *John Hancock: Merchant King and American Patriot*. New York: John Wiley & Sons, 2000.

Websites

The Coming of the American Revolution. www.masshist.org/revolution

Boston 1775. www.boston1775.blogspot.com

Founders Online. National Archives and Records Administration. founders.archives.gov

John Hancock's Letterbook (Business). Hancock Family Papers. nrs.harvard.edu/urn-3:HBS.Baker.GEN:5028297-2011

Journal of the American Revolution. www.allthingsliberty.com

Letters of Delegates to Congress 1774–1789. Library of Congress. memory.loc.gov/ammem/amlaw/lwdg.html

Visit

Many historical sites and items appearing in this book have been preserved for the public to visit. Here are a few:

The Hancock-Clarke House, Lexington, MA

Old South Meeting House, Boston, MA

Old State House, Boston, MA (*Hancock's red velvet suit*)

Minute Man National Historical Park, Lexington and Concord, MA (*"Hancock" cannon*)

Bunker Hill Monument, Boston, MA (*"Adams" cannon*)

Dorothy Quincy Homestead, Quincy, MA (*Hancock's golden carriage*)

Museum of Fine Arts, Boston, MA (*John Singleton Copley portraits of Hancock and Adams*)

Source Notes for Quotations

"at any price"

John Hancock to Lamar, Hill, and Bissett, July 23, 1765. Hancock Family Papers, Baker Library, Harvard Business School. https://hollisarchives.lib.harvard.edu/repositories/11/resources/7584 (accessed May 24, 2019).

"Illegal"

"An Act for Restraining and Preventing Several Unwarrantable Schemes . . .," *The Statutes at Large: From the Third Year of the Reign of King George the Second . . .* Vol. 6. (London: 1764, p. 430)

"The true object of loyalty . . ."

William Wells. *The Life and Public Services of Samuel Adams.* (Boston: 1865, p. 17)

"I am obliged to be pretty expensive."

John Hancock to Thomas Hancock, January 14, 1761. *Proceedings of the Massachusetts Historical Society,* Vol. 43. (Boston: 1910, p. 196)

"Very cruel"

John Hancock to Barnards and Harrison, April 5, 1765. Hancock Family Papers. See citation above.

"We must submit to higher powers"

John Hancock to Barnard and Harrison, May 13, 1765. Hancock Family Papers. See citation above.

"I seldom meddle with politics."

John Hancock to Thomas Pownall, July 6, 1765. Microfilm edition of the Hancock Family Papers, Massachusetts Historical Society.

"unconstitutional" and "alarming"

Records Relating to the Early History of Boston, Vol. 16. (Boston: 1886, p. 155)

"to declare our greatest dissatisfaction . . ."

The Writings of Samuel Adams, Vol. 1. (p. 10)

"To lose my property, if not my life."

John Hancock to Barnard and Harrison, October 14, 1765. Hancock Family Papers. See citation above.

"first"

Boston Gazette, May 19, 1766. (p. 3)

"I will not be a slave . . ."

John Hancock to Jonathan Barnard, October 21, 1765. Hancock Family Papers. See citation above.

"The town has done a wise thing . . ."
"Mr. Hancock was the delight . . ."

John Adams to William Tudor Sr., June 1, 1817. Founders Online, National Archives.

"In all cases whatsoever"

"An Act for the Better Securing the Dependency of His Majesty's Dominions in America upon the Crown and Parliament of Great Britain." *The Statutes at Large: From the Magna Charta . . .,* Vol. 27. (London: 1767, p. 20)

"horrid massacre"

A committee of the Town of Boston to Benjamin Franklin, July 13, 1770. *The Writings of Samuel Adams,* Vol. 1. (p. 10)

"affectionate friend"
"most valuable"
"the highest applause."

Samuel Adams to John Hancock, May 11, 1770. *The Writings of Samuel Adams,* Vol. 2. (p. 9)

"Cooking up paragraphs . . ."

John Adams's diary, September 3, 1769. Adams Family Papers: An Electronic Archive. Massachusetts Historical Society. http://www.masshist.org/digitaladams/archive/browse/diaries_by_number.php (accessed May 29, 2019).

"Hard at work writing . . ."

The Life and Public Services of Samuel Adams, Vol. 1. (p. 203)

"Every dip of his pen . . ."

John Adams's diary, September 21, 1775. Adams Family Papers: An Electronic Archive. Massachusetts Historical Society. http://www.masshist.org/digitaladams/archive/browse/diaries_by_number.php (accessed May 29, 2019).

"an idol of the mob"

Joseph Harrison to Lord Rockingham, June 17, 1768. Quoted in D. H. Watson, "Joseph Harrison and the Liberty Incident." *The William and Mary Quarterly,* Vol. 20, no. 4. (October 1963, p. 589)

"This meeting can do nothing more"

The Life and Public Service of Samuel Adams, Vol. 2. (p. 122)

"Let every man do what is right"

Benjamin Bussey Thatcher, *Traits of the Tea Party; Being a Memoir of George R. T. Hewes.* (New York: 1835, p. 178)

"Punish Hancock, Adams"

Proceedings and Debates of the British Parliaments Respecting North America, 1754–1783, Vol. 4. (New York: 1982, p. 136)

"The town of Boston ought to be . . ."

The Parliamentary History of England from the Earliest Period to the Year 1803, Vol. 17. (London: 1813, p. 1178)

"All should be united . . ."

The Committee of Correspondence of Boston to the Committee of Correspondence of Philadelphia, May 13, 1774. *The Writings of Samuel Adams*, Vol. 3. (p. 110)

"It is our duty at all hazards . . ."

Samuel Adams to James Warren, March 31, 1774. *The Writings of Samuel Adams*, Vol. 3. (p. 93)

"Be ready to take the field . . ."

John Hancock, *An Oration; Delivered March 5, 1774*. (Boston: Edes and Gill, 1774. p. 17)

"daring spirit of resistance"

King's Speech, November 30, 1774. *The Parliamentary History of England from the Earliest Period to the Year 1803*, Vol. 18. (p. 33)

"the most obnoxious of the leaders"

General Gage to Lord Dartmouth, January 18, 1775. Thomas Gage, *The Correspondence of General Thomas Gage*, Vol. 1. (New Haven: 1931, p. 390)

"The most notorious offenders . . . Hancock, Adams"

Benjamin Franklin, *A Method of Humbling Rebellious American Vassals*, May 21, 1774. Founders Online, National Archives.

"Come in, Revere . . ."

Elias Phinney, *History of the Battle at Lexington*. (Boston: 1825, p. 17)

"The regulars are coming out"

Testimony of Sergeant William Monroe, March 7, 1825. *History of the Battle at Lexington*. (p. 33)

"That is not our business."

"Reminiscences by Gen. Wm. H. Sumner," *The New England Historical and Genealogical Register*, Vol. 8. (Boston: 1854, p. 187)

"If I had my musket . . ."

Testimony of Sergeant William Monroe. *History of the Battle at Lexington*. (p. 34)

"gathering like a snowball"

Silas Deane to Elizabeth Deane, May 12, 1775. Paul H. Smith, ed., *Letters of Delegates to Congress*, Vol. 1. (Library of Congress: 1976, p. 346)

"Of course . . . first in the procession"
"No person could possibly be . . ."

John Hancock to Dorothy Quincy, May 7, 1775. New England Historic Genealogical Society, *The New England Historical and Genealogical Register*, Vol. 19. (Boston: 1865, p. 135)

"I do hereby in his Majesty's name . . ."

Massachusetts Governor Thomas Gage. *A Proclamation: Whereas the Infatuated Multitudes Who Have Long Suffered Themselves . . .* (New York: 1775). Library of Congress. www.loc.gov/item/rbpe.03801700/.

"fine salmon"
"get in the carriage and come over . . ."

"Incidents in the Life of John Hancock as Related by Dorothy Quincy Hancock Scott, From the Diary of General William H. Sumner." *The Magazine of American History with Notes and Queries*, Vol. 19. (January–June 1888, p. 504)

"sudden arrest, if not assassination . . ."

Rev. Jonas Clarke, *A Sermon, Preached at Lexington, April 19, 1776*. (Boston: Powars and Willis, 1776)

"It was too late . . ."

"Colonial Correspondence on the Boston Port Bill," Fourth Series, Massachusetts Historical Society Collections, IV. (p. 372)

"whenever the army . . ."

Arthur B. Tourtellot, *Lexington and Concord*. (New York: 1959, p. 51)